W9-BYQ-781

DISCOVERING SOUTH AMERICA
History, Politics, and Culture

PARAGUAY

BOLIVIA

Capitán Pablo Lagerenza

20°S

General Eugenio A. Garay

Fuerte
Olimpo

PARAGUAY

BRAZIL

22°S

Doctor Pedro P. Peña

Yacaré Norte River

Verde River

Pedro Juan
Caballero

Tropic of Capricorn

Pozo Colorado

Concepción

Monte Lindo River

24°S

San Pedro

Salto del
Guairá

Paraguay River

ARGENTINA

Asunción

Coronel
Oviedo

San Lorenzo

Ciudad
del Este

Villarrica

26°S

Parana River

N

W   E

S

Tebicuary River

Pilar

0   50   100 Miles

Encarnación

0   50   100 Kilometers
Oblique Conic Conformal Projection

28°S

62°W   60°W   58°W   56°W   54°W

DISCOVERING SOUTH AMERICA
History, Politics, and Culture

PARAGUAY

Roger E. Hernández

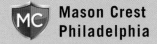
Mason Crest
Philadelphia

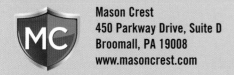

Mason Crest
450 Parkway Drive, Suite D
Broomall, PA 19008
www.masoncrest.com

Printed and bound in the United States of America.

CPSIA Compliance Information: Batch #DSA2015.
For further information, contact Mason Crest at 1-866-MCP-Book.

First printing
1 3 5 7 9 8 6 4 2

Library of Congress Cataloging-in-Publication Data
        on file at the Library of Congress

        ISBN: 978-1-4222-3301-6 (hc)
        ISBN: 978-1-4222-8644-9 (ebook)

Discovering South America: History, Politics, and Culture series ISBN: 978-1-4222-3293-4

DISCOVERING SOUTH AMERICA: History, Politics, and Culture

Argentina	**Chile**	**Guyana**	**Suriname**	**South America:**
Bolivia	**Colombia**	**Paraguay**	**Uruguay**	Facts & Figures
Brazil	**Ecuador**	**Peru**	**Venezuela**	

Table of Contents

KEY ICONS TO LOOK FOR:

Words to Understand: These words with their easy-to-understand definitions will increase the reader's understanding of the text, while building vocabulary skills.

Sidebars: This boxed material within the main text allows readers to build knowledge, gain insights, explore possibilities, and broaden their perspectives by weaving together additional information to provide realistic and holistic perspectives.

Research Projects: Readers are pointed toward areas of further inquiry connected to each chapter. Suggestions are provided for projects that encourage deeper research and analysis.

Text-Dependent Questions: These questions send the reader back to the text for more careful attention to the evidence presented there.

Series Glossary of Key Terms: This back-of-the book glossary contains terminology used throughout this series. Words found here increase the reader's ability to read and comprehend higher-level books and articles in this field.

Discovering South America

James D. Henderson

SOUTH AMERICA is a cornucopia of natural resources, a treasure house of ecological variety. It is also a continent of striking human diversity and geographic extremes. Yet in spite of that, most South Americans share a set of cultural similarities. Most of the continent's inhabitants are properly termed "Latin" Americans. This means that they speak a Romance language (one closely related to Latin), particularly Spanish or Portuguese. It means, too, that most practice Roman Catholicism and share the Mediterranean cultural patterns brought by the Spanish and Portuguese who settled the continent over five centuries ago.

Still, it is never hard to spot departures from these cultural norms. Bolivia, Peru, and Ecuador, for example, have significant Indian populations who speak their own languages and follow their own customs. In Paraguay the main Indian language, Guaraní, is accepted as official along with Spanish. Nor are all South Americans Catholics. Today Protestantism is making steady gains, while in Brazil many citizens practice African religions right along with Catholicism and Protestantism.

South America is a lightly populated continent, having just 6 percent of the world's people. It is also the world's most tropical continent, for a larger percentage of its land falls between the tropics of Cancer and Capricorn than is the case with any other continent. The world's driest desert is there, the Atacama in northern Chile, where no one has ever seen a drop of rain fall. And the world's wettest place is there too, the Chocó region of Colombia, along that country's border with Panama. There it rains almost every day. South America also has some of the world's highest mountains, the Andes,

A Paraguayan fan celebrates a soccer victory in Asunción.

and its greatest river, the Amazon.

So welcome to South America! Through this colorfully illustrated series of books you will travel through 12 countries, from giant Brazil to small Suriname. On your way you will learn about the geography, the history, the economy, and the people of each one. Geared to the needs of teachers and students, each volume contains book and web sources for further study, a chronology, project and report ideas, and even recipes of tasty and easy-to-prepare dishes popular in the countries studied. Each volume describes the country's national holidays and the cities and towns where they are held. And each book is indexed.

You are embarking on a voyage of discovery that will take you to lands not so far away, but as interesting and exotic as any in the world.

(Opposite) Iguazú Falls, located at the point where Argentina, Brazil, and Paraguay meet, is a popular tourist destination. (Right) Adult and baby capybaras. These aquatic South American mammals are the world's largest rodents. Adults can weigh 150 pounds (68 kilograms).

1 "An Island Surrounded by Land"

PARAGUAY HAS BEEN described as an island surrounded by land. It is blocked from the sea by its neighbors—Argentina, Bolivia, and Brazil—and is more than 400 miles (644 kilometers) from the nearest coast. It is a country of stark contrasts, divided by the Paraguay River into two distinct geographic regions: the Región Oriental in the east, with an area of about 61,700 square miles (159,741 sq km), and the larger Chaco in the west, made up of more than 95,000 square miles (245,955 sq km).

Along the border with Brazil, the Región Oriental is bounded by two mountain chains, the Cordillera de Amambay and the Cordillera de Mbaracayú (which are better known internationally by their Brazilian names, the Serra de Amambaí and the Serra de Maracajú, respectively). These low rolling hills rise to an average height of 1,500 feet (458 meters) and are covered with evergreen forest. Tall semi-tropical trees, ferns, and grass-

The capuchin monkey is one of many exotic species in Paraguay.

es provide a home for species such as the capuchin monkey and the harpy eagle. There are exotic flowers, such as the *brunfelsia*, or Paraguay jasmine. However, more than 12 million acres (4.85 million hectares) have already been destroyed by *deforestation*. Environmentalists fear that Paraguay's forests may soon be gone.

West of the Brazilian border the hills flatten out into grasslands irrigated by the country's two major rivers, the Paraguay and the Paraná, and their *tributaries*. Spectacular waterfalls abound. Paraguay's major cities, nearly all its industry, and much of its *agriculture* are in the fertile valleys of this region. The Paraná River forms the country's southeastern border with Brazil and Argentina.

Words to Understand in this Chapter

agriculture—the practice of growing crops or raising farm animals.
deforestation—the cutting down of forests for lumber or to clear the land for farming.
endemic—native to a particular area and existing nowhere else.
predator—an animal that survives by preying on other animals.
tributaries—streams that feed larger bodies of water, such as rivers or lakes.

Water hyacinths grow along the Paraguay River, the fifth-longest waterway in South America.

Across the Paraguay River, the Chaco region is a flat, featureless plain that makes up nearly two-thirds of the country's area but holds less than 5 percent of its population. It starts out as marshland in the Lower Chaco, closest to the river. The Estero Patiño, the largest swamp in the country, is located there. Further west, near the border with Bolivia, is the Upper Chaco. The land here is drier, covered by parched plains or scrub forest with dwarf trees and small bushes. The Pilcomayo River, the longest tributary of the Paraguay River, runs from Bolivia to near Asunción—Paraguay's capital city—then continues south. It forms Paraguay's southern border with Argentina.

Climate

Because Paraguay is located in the Southern Hemisphere, it experiences summer when residents of the United States are in the midst of winter; similarly, Paraguay's winter coincides with America's summer. In Paraguay,

Quick Facts: The Geography of Paraguay

Location: landlocked in South America, with Argentina to the south, Bolivia to the north, and Brazil to the east.

Area: (about the size of California)
   total: 157,046 square miles (406,750 sq km)
   land: 153,398 square miles (397,300 sq km)
   water: 3,649 square miles (9,450 sq km)

Borders: Argentina, 1,168 miles (1,880 km); Bolivia, 466 miles (750 km); Brazil, 802 miles (1,291 km).

Climate: subtropical to temperate.

Terrain: broad plateaus and low wooded hills in the Región Oriental, east of the Paraguay River; west of the Paraguay River, the Chaco is a plain—semi-dry in parts, marshy in others.

Elevation extremes:
   lowest point: junction of Paraguay and Paraná Rivers, 151 feet (46 meters).
   highest point: Cerro Pero, 2,762 feet (842 meters).

Natural hazards: floods in the summer, droughts in the winter.

Source: CIA World Factbook 2015.

summer lasts from October to March, and winter from May to August. April features fall-like weather, whereas September is Paraguay's spring month.

The Región Oriental has a subtropical climate. Its summers are warm. The average summer temperature in Asunción, for example, is about 80°F (27°C). During the Región Oriental's mild winter season, the average temperature in Asunción is 63°F (18°C), though temperatures occasionally reach the freezing mark. Rainfall is substantial, between 50 and 60 inches (127–152 centimeters) annually, and evenly distributed throughout the year.

In the Chaco the weather is tropical. Temperatures stay warm most of the year, sometimes climbing to 100°F (38°C). The most important seasonal difference in the Chaco is the amount of rainfall, not the temperature. In the summer months rainfall is so heavy it can cause floods, while the winter is plagued by frequent droughts.

Wildlife

A variety of wildlife lives in the semi-tropical forests of the Región Oriental and throughout the Chaco. Mammalian *predators* include jaguars, cougars, the Paraguayan fox, and the long-legged maned wolf. Among their prey are deer, armadillos, the guanaco (a relative of the llama), and the capybara, a large rodent *endemic* to South America. In the Chaco lives the Chacoan peccary, a species of wild pig believed extinct for thousands of years until it was discovered in 1975.

Reptiles include various kinds of lizards and iguanas, the alligator-like *yacaré*, and poisonous snakes. There is much bird life; parrots, toucans, ibises, eagles, and an ostrich-like bird called the rhea make their homes in Paraguay, as do various birds that breed in North America and fly south to the region for the winter.

Twelve mammal species, an equal number of bird species, and three reptile species are on the endangered list.

TEXT-DEPENDENT QUESTIONS

1. What three countries surround Paraguay?
2. What flat, featureless plain makes up nearly two-thirds of Paraguay's area?
3. What is the climate of the Región Oriental?

(Opposite) The remains of a Jesuit mission near present-day Encarnación. Spanish Jesuits arrived in Paraguay during the 17th century, spreading the Roman Catholic religion among the natives. (Right) A 19th-century illustration depicts scenes from mission life. Today an estimated 90 percent of Paraguayans are Roman Catholic.

2 Independence, Isolation, and Conflict

THE FIRST INHABITANTS of Paraguay were American Indians, most of whom belonged to related tribes that spoke the Guaraní language. *Nomads*, they survived by hunting and fishing. The largest of the tribes, the Guaranís themselves, were the most advanced.

Their world changed with the arrival of explorers from Spain and Portugal. The first European to set foot in Paraguay was Alejo García, a Portuguese explorer who landed on the coast of what is now Argentina in 1516 with a Spanish expedition. Indians slaughtered most of the Europeans. García and some followers lived in hiding until 1524, when they made their way inland near the site of present-day Asunción.

The region that today is Paraguay was not settled by Europeans until 1537, when the Spaniard Juan de Salazar founded a fort. Because it was the day of the Catholic Feast of the Assumption, Salazar named the outpost Asunción. The city became a provincial capital.

To encourage more settlers, the king of Spain granted large areas of land to colonists. In return, the settlers were supposed to care for the Indians living on the lands and convert them to Christianity. But the colonists took advantage, turning the Indians into virtual slaves. Abuses against the Indians angered many in Spain, including leaders of the powerful order of Catholic priests known as the *Jesuits*. With the backing of King Philip III, the Jesuits established their own settlements starting in the early 1600s. There Indians lived freely in communes run by Jesuit missionaries. The priests didn't just teach Christianity. They also showed the natives how to read and write Spanish and work in trades such as agriculture, leather making, and cloth making. Eventually 14,000 Jesuits lived with 100,000 Indians in some 30 missions, which were self-reliant and so successful that they became like a coun-

Words to Understand in this Chapter

armistice—in wartime, a final agreement of cease-fire.
impeachment—the process of charging a public official with crimes or misconduct in office.
Jesuits—Roman Catholic priests whose order, the Society of Jesus, was founded in the 16th century to perform educational and missionary work.
nomads—a group of people who have no fixed residence but move from place to place.
telegraph—a system for communicating over long distances through the transmission of electrical signals over wire.

try within a country. Their Indian armies, led by priests, defeated slave raiders from Brazil and landowners from Asunción who wanted to take over.

But the enemies kept trying. The Jesuits' power alarmed Charles III, Spain's new king. In 1767 he expelled the order from all of the Spanish Empire. The missions were taken over by people who mismanaged them and once again turned Indians into forced laborers.

Independence and Other Problems

Much as the people living in England's American colonies eventually broke away from Great Britain, the people living in Spanish colonies in South America fought for independence from Spain. One of the first uprisings took place in 1810 in Argentina. The Argentine revolutionaries sent an army to Paraguay hoping that people there would join them, but Paraguayans at first saw the soldiers as foreign invaders and fought them.

Nevertheless, the Paraguayans eventually agreed that Spanish rule should end. In May 1811, they rose in arms against the colonial government in Asunción and declared independence. However, once the new nation had won its independence, chaos followed. Because of its location deep inland, Paraguay lived apart from even the Spanish countries closest to it. Paraguayans knew little about self-government or about other nations. Powerful neighbors Brazil and Argentina thought the country weak and tried to interfere in its affairs.

Paraguay's response was to keep to itself for nearly 50 years. It found relative stability and, until the end of those five decades, freedom from foreign interference. But the country paid an enormous price in exchange for stability: rule by three dictators.

The first of the three was José Gaspar Rodríguez de Francia, known to Paraguayans as Doctor Francia, or simply as *El Supremo*. Dr. Francia suppressed all political activity, jailing his enemies or even having them killed. Subject to many death threats, he even forbade people to look at him when he traveled on the streets of Asunción.

During his dictatorship Dr. Francia turned Paraguay into a hermit nation. Fearful that his small country would be taken over by its larger neighbors, he sealed its borders, making it illegal for Paraguayans to leave and allowing just a handful of foreigners to visit. For the 26 years that Francia ruled, Paraguay had little contact with the outside world.

After Francia died there was a struggle for control of the government. By 1841 one man had come out on top—Carlos Antonio López.

López, too, established dictatorial rule. Like Francia, he jailed political opponents and sometimes had them killed. But he also began modernizing the country, opening Paraguay to the outside world. Engineers, doctors, and teachers from Europe helped Paraguay begin to catch up with surrounding countries. A railroad and a *telegraph* were built during López's 21-year rule.

War of the Triple Alliance

When Carlos Antonio López died in 1862, his son Francisco Solano López became the ruler of Paraguay. At the time, the country was in the midst of border disputes with Brazil and Argentina, and relations between the countries were tense. Francisco Solano López believed that Paraguay's army was strong enough to defeat Brazil and Argentina. So when Brazil invaded Uruguay—another small country in South America—in 1864, Solano López decided to act like the protector of little nations. He sent his army to attack the Brazilian forces in Uruguay.

This proved to be a tremendous mistake. The Paraguayan army was led by incompetent officers who had been appointed not for their military skills but because of their friendship with Solano López. Besides, Paraguay was far smaller than its neighbors. Brazil fought back. Argentina joined in, hoping to win a chunk of Paraguay for itself. Even Uruguay went to war against its supposed protector.

The war went disastrously for Paraguay. By the end of the fighting its pre-war population of about half a million had been reduced to approximately 220,000—with fewer than 28,000 adult males. In fact,

Francisco Solano López (1826–1870) took over as ruler of Paraguay after the death of his father in 1862. He soon involved his country in the War of the Triple Alliance. The war turned out badly for Paraguay, and the country would not recover for decades.

so many men were lost that, in one of the last battles of the war, Paraguay was forced to field an army composed of children—most of whom were slaughtered. Finally, in 1870, Brazilian soldiers overtook a retreating Francisco Solano López—the dictator who six years earlier had ignited the war—and killed him. The War of the Triple Alliance was over, but Paraguay's problems were not.

After the war Paraguay hit rock bottom. The economy was in ruins and there weren't enough men left to do the necessary work. Brazil and Argentina eventually sliced off a combined 55,000 square miles (142,395 sq km) of Paraguayan territory. Troops from these two countries occupied defeated Paraguay, remaining until 1876. And even after the soldiers left, Argentina and Brazil continued to interfere in Paraguayan politics. Governments came and went, depending on the support of the foreign powers.

Yet this bleak era gave birth to two political parties, the Liberal Party and the Colorado Party. Those two parties still dominate Paraguayan politics.

General Bernardino Caballero founded the Colorado Party, which controlled Paraguay for most of the period between 1880 and 1904. In 1904 Benigno Ferreira, a Liberal, defeated the Colorados in a civil war, with Argentinean support. For the next three decades, Liberals ruled.

Then Paraguay again went to war against a foreign enemy.

The Chaco War

Paraguay and Bolivia (the only other landlocked country in South America) both claimed the Chaco region. They believed it contained oil.

In 1932 Bolivian troops attacked a Paraguayan fort, and the war was on. Paraguay would lose more than 35,000 men in the fighting, but, led by a highly capable military commander, General José Félix Estigarribia, it won nearly every battle until an *armistice* in 1935. In the peace treaty signed three years later, Paraguay got three-quarters of the disputed territory, including a portion that had been Bolivia's.

General Estigarribia was imprisoned briefly the year after the war ended, by officers who wanted to install a government modeled on the Fascist regime of Italy's Benito Mussolini. That experiment failed, and by 1939 Estigarribia had become Paraguay's president. He didn't rule for long, however; in 1940 he was killed in a plane crash.

General Higinio Morínigo then took power. He survived a series of social upheavals and unsuccessful attempts to seize the government before finally being ousted in 1949. Five years of uprisings and violent changes of government followed Morínigo's overthrow. In the midst of the chaos, Paraguay once again fell prey to a strongman who brought order but was merciless to opponents.

Officials from Argentina witness the signing of the peace treaty that ended the Chaco War, fought between Paraguay and Bolivia, in July 1938. Paraguay received three-quarters of the disputed Chaco territory as a result of the peace settlement.

The Stroessner Years

With the backing of the Colorados and the army, General Alfredo Stroessner grabbed power in 1954 and held it for nearly 35 years, longer than any leader in Paraguay's history.

General Alfredo Stroessner, ruler of Paraguay from 1954 until 1989, was perhaps the most influential Paraguayan leader of the 20th century. His accomplishments included construction of the Itaipú Dam on the Paraná River. However, Stroessner brutally suppressed all opposition and allowed Paraguay to become a refuge for war criminals from Nazi Germany.

Like Francia and the Lópezes in the previous century, Stroessner permitted no political opposition. As his predecessors had done, he imprisoned thousands and had other political enemies killed. But Stroessner opened up Paraguay to the world more than it had ever been previously, with both good and bad results. On the negative side, this descendant of German immigrants allowed his nation to become a hiding place for Nazis. On the positive side, in 1973 he signed a treaty with Brazil for the creation of the Itaipú Dam. Located on the Paraguay-Brazil border, this gigantic hydroelectric project created tens of thousands of jobs and brought electricity to areas of Paraguay that had long gone without power.

In 1983 Stroessner "won" a seventh presidential election. But a faction of the

Colorados that sought more freedom and democracy challenged him. General Andrés Rodríguez aligned himself with the moderates and overthrew the dictator in 1989. Stroessner fled to Brazil, where he died in 2006.

Democracy Arrives

Rodríguez promised a free press, freedom of expression, and free elections. A few months after Stroessner escaped, the election was held. Rodríguez won. It was the beginning of democracy in Paraguay. In 1991 voters elected a new congress with both Colorado and Liberal members. In 1992 a new democratic constitution went into effect. And one year later Colorado candidate Juan Carlos Wasmosy became Paraguay's first freely elected civilian president.

But democracy came under attack. In 1996 General Lino Oviedo attempted a coup d'etat. He failed and was imprisoned. But a supporter of his, Raúl Cubas, won the presidential election in 1998. Upon taking office, Cubas released Oviedo from prison and refused to send him back even after the Supreme Court ruled that he had to. In the turmoil that followed, Vice President Luis María Argaña, who opposed Cubas and Oviedo, was assassinated.

It appeared that Paraguay was headed for more chaos and yet another return to rule by a strongman. But in March 1999, Cubas resigned under threat of *impeachment*. Senate president Luis González Macchi, a Cubas opponent and his constitutionally designated replacement, was sworn in as the new president. González Macchi built a coalition government that included the Liberal Party as well as members of the anti-Oviedo faction of the Colorados.

President Fernando Lugo was removed from office in 2012.

Beginning in 2001 Paraguay also became embroiled in the war against terrorism. After the September 11 attack on the World Trade Center and the Pentagon, U.S. officials asked the Paraguayan government to crack down on fundraising allegedly carried on by Islamic extremists in the "Triple Frontier" area, where the borders of Paraguay, Argentina, and Brazil meet.

In July 2002, violent protests and an apparent coup attempt rocked the Paraguayan government. President González Macchi accused General Oviedo, who was living in exile in Brazil, of masterminding the unsuccessful uprising. Oviedo appeared to have broad support from impoverished residents of Paraguay's countryside.

González Macchi endured several further attempts to remove him from office. After his divisive presidency ended in 2003, González Macchi was arrested for financial crimes.

Nicanor Duarte, González Macchi's successor, vowed to fight crime and corruption. His administration tackled the issues of voter fraud and unemployment. Drug-related crime, including kidnappings, was a major problem during his presidency.

Many Paraguayans were optimistic after the 2008 presidential elections, which indicated that the country was progressing into a multi-party democracy. A former bishop who promised to help the poor, Fernando Lugo became Paraguay's first president from outside the Colorado Party in 61 years. His election also marked the first time in Paraguay's history that power passed to an opposition party peacefully.

Horacio Cartes

Unfortunately, the Lugo administration was not without controversy and problems. In 2010, the military was sent to northern Paraguay to track down a rebel group that was carrying out violent attacks. In 2012, when 17 people were killed in a land eviction, the national assembly reacted by impeaching President Lugo and removing him from office. Lugo's vice president, Federico Franco, was sworn in to complete the rest of Mr Lugo's term. Most of Paraguay's South American neighbors denounced this action as a coup. Franco agreed to step down when elections for a new president were scheduled for April 2013.

In the presidential election, Horacio Cartes, a businessman and candidate of the Colorado Party, was elected president with 46 percent of the vote.

TEXT-DEPENDENT QUESTIONS

1. What Roman Catholic religious order settled in Paraguay during the 17th century?
2. What 19th century dictator made Paraguay a "hermit nation?"
3. Who is the longest-serving ruler in Paraguay's history?

(Opposite) The Itaipú Dam is the largest in the world. Its hydroelectric plant produces much more than enough energy for Paraguay's needs; 98 percent of the power generated at the plant is sold to other countries, particularly Brazil. (Right) Harvest of sugarcane in San Pedro.

3 Agriculture and Hydroelectricity: The Economy

COMPARED WITH THE United States—and even with the other nations of South America—Paraguay is a poor country. According to statistics compiled by the World Bank, its 2014 *gross domestic product (GDP)*—a measure of the total size of a nation's economy—was one of the smallest among South America's independent countries, ahead of only Guyana and Suriname. More important, though, only Guyana ranked behind Paraguay in GDP per capita. GDP per capita, which is calculated by dividing a nation's GDP by its population, represents each citizen's share of the national economy. So, on average, Paraguayans are poorer than almost all their neighbors. More than one in three Paraguayans was living below the poverty line in 2014.

The economy of Paraguay depends on agriculture, industrial processing of agricultural goods, and production of *hydroelectricity*. A large underground economy, based on the smuggling of goods for re-export to Brazil and Argentina, is important too. Mining is little developed. Paraguay has no known petroleum reserves, making it dependent on foreign oil.

Paraguay is a member of the Southern Cone Common Market (MERCOSUR), a *trading bloc* that also includes Argentina, Brazil, and Uruguay. In 2012 Paraguay was suspended from MERCOSUR due to the impeachment of President Lugo, which other Latin American leaders viewed as a coup. While Paraguay was suspended, Venezuela was admitted as the fifth member of MERCOSUR. Since being reinstated, Paraguay's leaders have moved to block Bolivia from joining MERCOSUR. Today, the MERCOSUR countries have more than 275 million inhabitants, making it the world's fourth-largest trade bloc. Nearly 60 percent of Paraguay's exports go to MERCOSUR countries, with the country's largest trade partner being Brazil.

Words to Understand in this Chapter

agribusinesses—corporations engaged in large-scale farming or food processing.
gross domestic product (GDP)—the total value of goods and services produced by a nation in a one-year period.
hydroelectricity—electricity generated from water power.
privatize—to turn a government-controlled business or industry over to independent owners.
tanneries—factories or workshops where animal hides are turned into leather.
trading bloc—a group of countries that engage in international trade together, generally through a free trade agreement or other association.

Agriculture

A significant number of Paraguayans make a living from agriculture. In fact, more than one-quarter of the labor force is involved in the agricultural sector. Approximately 200,000 farm families grow what they need to feed themselves and not much else, with little participation in the broader economy.

A Paraguayan man stokes the fire under a brick kiln. Paraguay is one of the least developed nations in South America.

Larger farms produce enough to sell for domestic consumption and for export. Soybeans are an important crop. According to some estimates, by 2014 this crop accounted for nearly half of Paraguay's agricultural exports. It is a new crop in Paraguay, having been introduced only in the 1960s. Soybeans are grown mostly by huge *agribusinesses* owned by foreigners from Brazil or the United States.

From the time of the Jesuits, cotton has been an important crop in Paraguay. In the past, cotton was grown on small family farms using old methods. Some is still grown that way, but most cotton production has been taken over by agribusinesses, with their modern techniques and higher yields.

Industry

Paraguay is one of the least industrialized South American nations. Traditionally, manufacturing was carried out by small, family-run businesses. These types of facilities still provide processed food staples like bread, sugar, and dairy products. Locally owned metal shops and *tanneries* also dot the country.

In recent years, large foreign-owned companies have opened industrial plants to process cooking oil from soybeans or sunflower seeds. Paraguay also makes non-edible oils. These include tung oil, which is derived from tung nuts and is used in paints and furniture polish, and petitgrain oil, which is extracted from special oranges that are too bitter to eat but yield a fragrant substance for cosmetics, perfumes, and soaps. Oils are a major source of export sales.

Quick Facts: The Economy of Paraguay

Gross domestic product (GDP*):
$57.87 billion
GDP per capita: $8,400
Natural resources: hydropower, timber, iron ore, manganese, limestone.
Agriculture (19.9% of GDP): cotton, sugarcane, soybeans, corn, wheat, tobacco, cassava (manioc, tapioca), fruits, vegetables; beef, pork, eggs, milk; timber.
Industry (17.6% of GDP): sugar, cement, textiles, beverages, wood products, steel, base metals, electric power.
Services (62.5% of GDP): finance, transportation, communication, schools, hospitals, government agencies, tourism.

Inflation: 5.1%
Foreign trade:
Exports—$14.61 billion: soybeans, livestock feed, cotton, meat, edible oils, wood, leather.
Imports—$12.37 billion: road vehicles, consumer goods, tobacco, petroleum products, electrical machinery, tractors, chemicals, vehicle parts.
Currency exchange rate: 4,992 Paraguayan guarani = US $1 (2015).

*Gross domestic product (GDP) represents the total value of goods and services produced in a country during a particular year. All figures are 2014 estimates unless otherwise noted.
Source: CIA World Factbook 2015.

Manufacturing of yerba maté, a tea-like beverage considered Paraguay's national drink, is important. There are also meatpacking plants, cement factories, shoe and clothing makers, sawmills, and the recently *privatized* Acepar steel mill. A growing industry is the making of ethanol, a vehicle fuel Paraguay hopes will lessen its dependence on imported petroleum.

Hydroelectricity

A key economic development in Paraguay's history was the construction of hydroelectric power plants along the country's river borders with Brazil and

Argentina. These power plants allow the country to export more than 46 billion kilowatt-hours of electricity a year, yielding 35 percent of total government revenues. Paraguay is among the world's largest sellers of electric power.

The largest hydroelectric plant in the world is Itaipú, on the Paraná River. Electricity was first generated there in 1984 after expenditures of some $20 billion, most of which came from Brazil. Itaipú is breathtakingly huge. The dam is 643 feet (196 meters) tall, with a reservoir area of 870 square miles (2,252 sq km). Its 18 generators can put out 12,600 megawatts of power, nearly twice the capacity of Grand Coulee Dam, the largest dam in the United States. Paraguay gets about three-quarters of its electricity from Itaipú, but that is only 2 percent of the plant's total output. The rest is sold to Brazil.

Another large hydroelectric project in Paraguay is the Yacyreta Dam, a joint Paraguayan-Argentinean project. Yacyreta is located near the town of Encarnación. The dam was completed in 1994, but did not start producing electricity to its full capacity until 2011.

These vast hydroelectric projects have raised environmental concerns. For example, to build Itaipú, workers diverted the course of the Paraná River, flooded 407,724 acres (165,000 hectares) of habitat, and submerged the spectacular Guairá Falls.

Services

More than half of Paraguay's workers are employed in service jobs, including private and government services. This service sector accounts for over 60 percent of the nation's gross domestic product. Much of the business activity is related to the import of goods from Western Europe, Asia, and the

United States for re-export to Brazil and Argentina. In addition to the government-run Central Bank, Paraguay has a number of commercial multinational institutions that entered the country to help finance the massive hydroelectricity projects. There are also insurance companies and small, locally owned savings-and-loan associations.

Tourism is important too. In recent years, Paraguay has attracted more than 350,000 visitors annually. These tourists contribute over $700 million to the country's economy.

Less accountable is the "hidden" economy. Street vendors and owners of small businesses do not report their earnings. Smuggled computers, stereos, cameras, liquor, and perfumes are sold to Brazil and Argentina. These activities are illegal, so no one knows how much money is involved.

 TEXT-DEPENDENT QUESTIONS

1. What trade bloc is Paraguay a founding member of?
2. What is a leading agricultural crop for export?
3. What hydroelectric dam is located near the town of Encarnación?

(Opposite) Family members laugh during a picnic in San Pedro. Paraguay's population has grown to nearly 7 million people. (Right) Around 20,000 young Paraguayans congregate to celebrate the arrival of spring on a central street in Asunción.

4 Equal Parts Spanish and Guaraní: The Culture and People

THE PEOPLE OF BILINGUAL, bicultural Paraguay embrace both their Spanish and Indian heritage to an extent unequaled in any other Latin American nation. Countries such as Bolivia and Guatemala also have large populations that retained their Indian language and culture after the arrival of the Spanish in the 1500s. But Bolivia's Quechua-speakers and Guatemala's Mayan-speakers are poor and outside the mainstream. In Paraguay even the *elite* speak the Guaraní language. In fact, some studies indicate that a majority of Paraguayans prefer to speak the Indian language in their homes.

For Paraguayans, Guaraní is not only the language of home, it is also the language of culture. Popular music is sung in both Spanish and Guaraní; there are Guaraní dictionaries and websites, books and plays. However, all five daily newspapers in the capital are published in Spanish (although the largest, *ABC*, publishes a small Guaraní supplement), as is much television programming.

Guaraní's continuing importance in Paraguayan society is guaranteed by its deep roots in the nation's history. The Jesuit missionaries of the 17th and 18th centuries protected speakers of Guaraní from the cultural and physical destruction that Indians elsewhere experienced. After the end of the Jesuit era, at the urging of Dr. Francia, there were many marriages between Indians and white Spaniards of all social classes, creating a truly *mestizo* society. Today, knowing Guaraní is an essential part of the national identity, a way for Paraguayans to distinguish themselves from other Latin Americans.

Everyday Life

Families are at the center of life in Paraguay. For Paraguayans family includes not just parents and children, but also grandparents, uncles, aunts,

Words to Understand in this Chapter

dialect—an often regional variety of a language that has distinctive vocabulary, pronunciation, and grammar.

elite—a society's cultural, economic, or political leaders.

Mennonites—members of one of various Protestant groups with origins in 16th-century German and Dutch religious sects.

and cousins. Although they may not all live together under the same roof, Paraguayans tend to rely on these extended families for things like recreation, jobs, financial support in times of need, and even political allegiances. In the United States, by contrast, communities as a whole—including government agencies, social clubs, churches, private businesses, and political associations—play a more active role.

A Guaraní Indian wears a beaded necklace and red scarf. Though the Guaraní language is widely used in the country, only a small minority of Paraguay's population is full-blooded Guaraní; most of the people are of mixed Indian and Spanish heritage.

Like other residents of Latin countries, Paraguayans keep the tradition of the siesta. Around noontime, schools and businesses close and everybody goes home to rest and eat a big lunch with the family. Activities resume a couple of hours later.

Paraguayans love charcoal-grilled meats, simply seasoned with salt and pepper. Stews are also popular. There is *so'o-yosopy*, which means "meat soup" in Guaraní and is served with rice or noodles. Another traditional dish is *sopa paraguaya*, or Paraguayan soup—which is not actually a soup at all but a kind of fluffy corn cake.

Paraguayan children attend school at least until the age of 14. Classes run from 7 A.M. to 11 A.M., then schools close for two hours, reopening at 1

Quick Facts: The People of Paraguay

Population: 6,703,860

Ethnic groups: mestizo (mixed Spanish and Amerindian) 95%, other 5%.

Age structure:
0–14 years: 26.2%
15–64 years: 67.2%
65 years and over: 6.6%

Population growth rate: 1.19%

Birth rate: 16.66 births/1,000 population

Death rate: 4.64 deaths/1,000 population

Infant mortality rate: 20.75 deaths/1,000 live births

Life expectancy at birth: 76.8 years

Total fertility rate: 1.96 children born/woman

Religions: Roman Catholic 89.6%, Protestant 6.2%, other Christian 1.1%, other or unspecified 1.9%, none 1.1% (2002).

Languages: Spanish (official), Guarani (official).

Literacy (age 15 and older): 93.9% (2010).

All figures are 2014 estimates unless otherwise noted.
Source: CIA World Factbook 2014.

P.M. The school day concludes around 5 P.M. In the cities, most kids go on to high school. But in the countryside, where classrooms are overcrowded and children often have to travel long distances on bad roads to get to school, many drop out to work on the family farm.

Few Paraguayans attend college. The country has seven universities, all of which are located in Asunción. Universidad Nacional, the largest and oldest (founded in 1889), has branches, or satellite campuses, in other cities. There are also technical centers that offer training in commerce, industry, technology, or agriculture.

Paraguayans' tastes in music run from traditional Paraguayan folk songs to opera to rock. Pop singers famous in the United States are also famous in Paraguay. Performers from Paraguay and other Spanish-speaking countries are popular as well.

Many Paraguayans are passionate about soccer. Here, members of the national team (in red and white) compete against Bolivia.

Paraguayans are passionate about soccer. Children play whenever they get a chance, whether or not in organized leagues. Professional Paraguayan players are renowned throughout the world for *garra*, a never-say-die spirit. The national team has qualified for the World Cup tournament eight times, but has never done as well as South America's soccer giants, Brazil and Argentina. The most popular clubs in the domestic Paraguayan league are Olimpia, Cerro Porteño, and Club Libertad, all of which are based in Asunción. Olimpia and Cerro Porteño have each won the national club championship more than 30 times. Club Libertad dominated the early years of the 21st century, however, winning titles in 2002, 2003, 2006, 2007, 2008, 2009, and 2010. Olimpia has won the Copa Libertadores, which is the South American club championship, three times: in 1979, 1990, and 2002.

Religion plays a role in Paraguayan life, but the Catholic Church (to which most Paraguayans belong) is not as influential as it is elsewhere in

The National Cathedral of Paraguay, a Roman Catholic church, is located in Asunción.

South America. Other religious groups include the *Mennonites*—with roots in Germany—and evangelical Protestant denominations.

Indians

Even with the pride that Paraguayans take in all things Guaraní, Indians are often looked down upon by the mestizo majority, and they are more likely to live in poverty than other Paraguayans. Indians, in turn, often keep apart from the national culture.

Actually, there aren't many people in Paraguay who view themselves as Indian. Fully 95 percent of the population is mestizo, with the remainder split between Indians and whites. By some estimates, there are fewer than 70,000 Indians in the country—compared with more than 4 million each in Bolivia and Guatemala, two other Latin American countries having strong Indian influence.

Most Indians speak a *dialect* of Guaraní different from the one used in the rest of society, which segregates them further. In addition, 20,000 to 25,000 people speak one of a dozen other languages belonging to the Mascoian, Zamucoan, or Mataco native groups, unrelated to Guaraní.

Immigrant Groups in Paraguay

Some 12,000 immigrants arrived in Paraguay between the 1880s and the early 1900s, as the government tried to replace the tens of thousands of men killed in the War of the Triple Alliance. Nearly 9,000 of the immigrants hailed from Italy, Germany, France, or Spain. Others came from neighboring Latin American countries and the Arab world. Another small wave of immigrants from Germany and Japan arrived from the 1920s to the 1940s. A third wave came in the 1970s and 1980s.

Hundreds of thousands of Brazilian construction workers, engineers, and executives crossed into Paraguay during the 1970s and 1980s at the height of the hydroelectric building boom. Along the Brazilian border region, Portuguese has become a language of commerce, spoken by many people. Portuñol, a hybrid dialect of Portuguese and Spanish, is heard too.

German immigrants arrived in the 1880s to farm in the Chaco. Today many Paraguayans speak German. Another 38,000 Mennonites, who speak a German dialect, built agricultural colonies in the central Chaco between the 1920s and the 1940s. Mennonites still have a distinct identity, leading rural lives in the Chaco wilderness.

Like Paraguay's Mennonites, Japanese immigrants—most of whom arrived in the 1930s after the government opened up the country to Asian immigration—built agricultural colonies in the Chaco. For years they, too, lived apart from the rest of society.

This 1879 painting by the South American artist Juan Manuel Blanes (1830–1901), titled *The Paraguayan*, depicts a downcast woman contemplating the devastation of the War of the Triple Alliance.

In contrast to the agricultural Japanese, ethnic Chinese and Koreans tend to live in the cities. Most settled in Asunción or Ciudad del Este during the 1960s, specializing in the import and sale of electronic goods manufactured in Asia. A population of Arab origin also takes part in the import-export business.

Music, Arts, and Literature

Paraguayan folk songs feature Spanish-influenced rhythms and melodies, played on guitars and harps. Styles of music include the fast-paced *galopa* and the slower *guaraña*. The most famous composer of traditional Paraguayan music was Agustín Barrios (1885–1944). Although his music was Spanish in form, he often performed in Guaraní costume, singing bilingual lyrics.

Among handicrafts, the best-known

Paraguayan product is *ñandutí*, finely embroidered linen lace used in place-mats and shawls. *Aho-poi*, a white cotton cloth for dresses, shirts, and ponchos, is also typical. Carved wood statues of religious figures are another traditional handicraft, dating back to the Jesuit missions. Artisans also adorn leather with intricate designs.

The leading cultural center in Asunción is the Ateneo Paraguayo, which sponsors lectures, art exhibits, and concerts. The Teatro Guaraní offers plays in that language, including translations of classic works from Spanish as well as other European languages.

In literature, books and dictionaries are available in both of the national tongues. The most famous Paraguayan author is novelist Augusto Roa Bastos (1917–2005). His best-known work is *Yo el Supremo*, a novel of life during the regime of José Gaspar Rodríguez de Francia.

TEXT-DEPENDENT QUESTIONS
1. What is the largest and oldest university in Paraguay?
2. What is the average life expectancy at birth for a citizen of Paraguay?
3. Where is the main Mennonite community in Paraguay located?

(Opposite) Slum dwellings in Asunción. Many of the people living in these shanties have moved to the city in hopes of finding work. (Right) A steam locomotive travels the rails between Asunción and Encarnación. The railroad, which was completed in 1909, contributed greatly to Encarnación's development in the first half of the 20th century.

5 A Nation of Rural Communities and Small Cities

LARGE NUMBERS OF Paraguayans have begun living in cities, rather than on farms, only relatively recently. Today, 56 percent live in urban areas and 44 percent in rural areas. Still, the only place in Paraguay that comes close to qualifying as a big city is the nation's capital, Asunción; its *metropolitan area* is home to about a million residents.

Not surprisingly, the cities are much more developed than the country-side. For instance, nearly all the residents of Asunción have electricity and running water, but in rural areas just 83 percent of the people have access to healthy drinking water and only 76 percent have electricity at home.

Outside of Asunción, the largest cities in Paraguay are Ciudad del Este and Encarnación.

Asunción

In 2015, nearly 500 years after its founding, Asunción boasted an estimated population of 512,000. The capital retains a sleepy colonial atmosphere, with red-tiled roofs, whitewashed mansions, old plazas, and flower-filled interior patios.

Settlement dates from August 15, 1537, when the Spaniard Juan de Salazar founded a fort on a *bluff* overlooking the Paraguay River. The city grew into the seat of government for Spanish colonies as far away as the Río de la Plata, in present-day Argentina. But a royal order in 1617 created a separate provincial government in Buenos Aires, and Asunción became a backwater of the Spanish Empire. By 1747, when it was raided by Indians, the town had a mere 5,000 residents.

In the early 19th century Asunción became the center of the independence movement. The Casa de la Independencia, where revolutionaries met to plot the uprising, is now home to a museum featuring historical items from that period. After independence the population grew. But the War of the Triple Alliance devastated Asunción. Bombardment by Brazilian warships

Words to Understand in this Chapter

bluff—a high cliff that overlooks a river or waterway.
metropolitan area—the area that includes a large city as well as the nearby suburbs that are economically and socially dependent on the city.

forced an evacuation in 1868. The surviving population of 18,000 consisted mostly of war widows and children.

The city was slow to rebuild. Until the middle of the 20th century there were few paved roads, and most residents had no electricity or running water.

Among noteworthy buildings are the Palacio del Gobierno (Palace of Government), the Pantheon of Heroes (where national heroes are buried), and the Catholic cathedral, which dates from 1687. The city has modern buildings as well, such as the downtown office towers built in the 1970s. Since that building boom the population has grown relatively slowly in the city itself, but the metropolitan area has exploded. Suburbs such as San Lorenzo, Luque, and Lambaré, once small farm

A view of the Paraguayan flag flying in front of government buildings in Asunción.

towns, have reached 100,000 inhabitants and are larger than any other city except Ciudad del Este.

Ciudad del Este

Founded as Puerto Stroessner in 1957, Ciudad del Este sits on the banks of the Paraná River, 200 miles (322 km) due east of Asunción. After the open-

Taxis in downtown Ciudad Del Este. Paraguay's second-largest city is located near the Brazilian border.

ing of the Friendship Bridge—which completed the first direct highway connection between Paraguay and Brazilian seaports in 1965—Ciudad del Este grew quickly. By 2015 the city's population had reached an estimated 222,000.

During the 1970s and 1980s construction of the nearby Itaipú hydroelectric plant and an increase in tourists visiting beautiful Iguazú Falls (also known by its Brazilian name, Iguaçu Falls) brought explosive growth, which in turn brought more road connections and still more growth. The old name of Puerto Stroessner was changed in 1989, the year Paraguay's longtime dictator was overthrown. Paraguay's second-largest city continues booming as an entry point for foreign goods that are re-exported—legally and illegally—to Brazil or Argentina.

The city has little in the way of cultural attractions and, being so new, no colonial architecture. But it has a bustling downtown and several huge air-conditioned malls full of electronics and other goods that are snapped up by visiting Brazilian tourists.

Encarnación

Historic Encarnación, with an estimated 2015 population of 67,100, was founded as a Jesuit mission in the early 1600s. The capital of the province of Itapúa, a farming region in the southeast of the country, Encarnación is 230 miles (370 km) southeast of Asunción and roughly the same distance southwest of Ciudad del Este.

The original mission, called Itapúa, no longer exists. But the town is just 20 miles (32 km) away from Trinidad, home to one of the largest and most impressive of Paraguay's surviving Jesuit missions. It has churches, crypts, and residences for priests and Indians, with beautiful stone carvings of religious motifs finished in great detail. A smaller mission, Jesús de Tavarangué, is six miles (about 10 km) from the city center.

Encarnación has since colonial times been a center of trade for agricultural goods. A rail link to Asunción completed in 1909 made the town even more important. Nearby farms include a Japanese settlement that grows cotton, soybeans, and vegetables.

The city has had its share of disasters. In 1927 a tornado destroyed much of Encarnación. In 1931 it was briefly taken over by anti-government rebels.

Today agriculture continues to be important to Encarnación, as does the Yacyreta hydroelectric plant near the city.

TEXT-DEPENDENT QUESTIONS

1. What are the three largest cities of Paraguay?
2. What was the original name of Ciudad del Este?

Paraguay has a number of national holidays to mark historical occasions, as well as many local fiestas to celebrate patron saints in small towns. Other South American nations have the same kinds of festivities, but in Paraguay the holidays are often influenced by the nation's Guaraní heritage.

January

Paraguayans start off each year with, of course, **New Year's Day** celebrations. They also follow the Latin custom of exchanging holiday gifts on January 6, **Three Kings Day**, when tradition says that the Magi brought gifts of incense, myrrh, and gold to the baby Jesus.

February

February 3 is the feast of **San Blas**, a saint popular among devout Catholics everywhere in Paraguay. The largest celebration is in Itá, where people attend big dinner-dances after Mass and a religious procession.

Depending on when Easter falls in a given year, February may also be the time for **Carnaval** (Carnival), the celebration before the solemn Catholic season of Lent. Among the most popular celebrations are those in Encarnación and Guayra, where floats, dancers, and musicians take over the streets. Around Carnaval time there are also separate celebrations such as **Areté Guazú** in Santa Teresita, featuring Guaraní costumes and masks.

March

The first of the month is **Heroes of the Fatherland**, when Paraguayans honor compatriots who died in war.

Holy Week, which can fall in March or April, is celebrated with religious processions on **Holy Thursday** and **Good Friday** and Mass on **Easter Sunday**.

April

Each year in Canindeyú during the month of April, there is an exposition of local agricultural and manufactured products and handicrafts.

May

Día del Trabajador (May 1), the internationally recognized May Day celebration honoring working men and women, is an official Paraguayan holiday.

Another official holiday, on May 15, is **Independence Day**, marking the end of colonial rule.

More local festivities include the **Alarcitas Handicrafts Fair** in Puno and trade fairs in Coronel Oviedo and Santa Rita.

June

On June 12, Paraguayans celebrate the anniversary of the **Chaco Armistice**, which ended Paraguay's victorious war against Bolivia.

Toward the end of the month is the **Verbena de San Juan**, a traditional national fiesta that includes food, music, and exhibitions such as walking on hot embers.

July

On July 20 the remote Chaco town of General Bruguez comes alive with a fiesta in honor of **Santa Librada**, another saint popular in Paraguay.

August

Mid-August has two of the most important nationwide observances. August 15 is not only the Catholic **Feast of the Assumption**, but also the anniversary of the **Founding of Asunción**. One day later is the **Day of the Child**, when schools are closed to honor children who died in a battle at the end of the War of the Triple Alliance.

Also in August the Mennonite community celebrates its major annual fiesta, the **Expo Trébol**, an agricultural exposition held on open fields between the Chaco towns of Loma Plata and Filadelfia.

September

The city of Concepción holds its annual **Trade Fair** in September, featuring a cattle exhibit. Also this month is one of the most popular events in the Chaco, the **Transchaco Rally**, which brings thousands of auto racing fans to the town of Mariscal Estigarribia. An annual **Alfalfa Festival** is held in the town of Sapucai in September, while the season's major religious fiesta honors the **Virgen de la Merced**, in the town of Puno.

The only true national holiday, however, is the anniversary of the **Battle of Boquerón** on September 29, commemorating a victory in the Chaco War.

October

The town of Encarnación holds an annual **International Choir Festival** this month, with concerts featuring choirs from several countries.

November

The town of Carapeguá holds the **Festival del Poyvi**, an arts, crafts, and music fair.

December

On December 8, pilgrims make their way to a religious sanctuary in the town of Caacupé to pay tribute to Paraguay's patron saint, **Our Lady of Caacupé**. The chapel dates from 1769. After this, people start preparing for **Christmas** celebrations. Families make a *pesebre*, a Nativity scene with the baby Jesus in the manger, which is lit with candles and adorned with aromatic coconut flowers. The *pesebre* is put under the Christmas tree, and on Christmas Eve family and friends gather before it to sing carols and pray.

 **Recipes**

Sopa Paraguaya (Cornbread)

(Serves 12)
3 big onions, chopped
1/2 cup lard
1 tbsp coarse salt
4 eggs
12 oz grated cheese
3 cups water
1 lb corn flour
1 cup milk
1 tbsp cream

Directions:
1. Simmer the onions and wait until they are cold again.
2. Stir in the lard, salt, and eggs. Add grated cheese and water. Slowly add flour, milk, and cream.
3. Put batter into a greased and floured baking dish.
4. Bake at 400°F for 1 hour.

Adapted from http://www.redparaguaya.com/recetas/sopa.htm

So'o-yosopy (Beef and Vegetable Soup)

2 medium onions, finely chopped
1 green bell pepper, finely chopped
4 medium tomatoes, peeled and chopped
2 lbs finely ground beef
8 cups cold water
2 tbsp vegetable oil
1/2 cup rice or vermicelli
Salt to taste
Grated Parmesan cheese

Directions:
1. Sauté the onions and pepper until soft. Add tomatoes and cook until well blended, about 5 minutes. Cool slightly.
2. Put ground beef into a saucepan. Stir in the sautéed onions, pepper, and tomatoes and the cold water. Bring to a boil over moderate heat, stirring with a wooden spoon.
3. Add the rice or noodles and simmer, still stirring, until tender, about 15 minutes.
4. Season to taste with salt. Sprinkle with grated cheese.

Adapted from www.onparaguay.com/recipe.html

Christmas Chicken

1 large roasting chicken
Juice of one lemon
2 garlic cloves, minced
1 onion, minced
1/2 cup white wine
1/2 cup red wine
1/2 cup sherry
4 tbsp butter

Stuffing:
1 chopped green apple
1/2 cup raisins
1/2 cup almonds
4 slices bacon, diced
1/2 cup ground beef
1/2 cup ground pork

Directions:
1. Place chicken in a roasting pan. Mix garlic, onion, and lemon juice and rub on chicken.
2. Pour wines over chicken and drizzle with melted butter.
3. Sauté stuffing ingredients in butter.
4. Bake chicken and stuffing separately in oven at 400°F until done.

Adapted from www.redparaguaya.com/recetas/pollodenavidad.htm

Empanadas Paraguayas (Meat Turnovers)

1/2 lb chopped beef
1 onion
1/2 bell pepper, minced
1 hard-boiled egg, chopped
2 tbsp raisins
6–8 olives, pitted and minced
1 lb wheat flour
1 fresh egg
Salt to taste
2 tbsp butter

Directions:
1. Sauté the chopped beef with the onions and pepper until brown.
2. Add the boiled egg, raisins, and olives and cook one or two minutes more. Set aside.
3. In a large container, mix the flour, egg, salt, and butter. Knead and spread out with rolling pin. Using a pastry cutter or a water glass, cut into 10–12 discs.
4. Place beef mixture in center of each disc and fold over. Press down on the edges of the half-moons with a fork to seal.
5. Cook in oven at 400°F for about 15 minutes or until golden.

Adapted from http://www.redparaguaya.com/recetas/empanadas.htm

Series Glossary

Amerindian—a term for the indigenous peoples of North, Central, and South America before the arrival of Europeans in the late 15th century.

Carnival—a popular festival in many South American countries, characterized by parades, dancing, and ornate costumes. It is celebrated just before the start of the Roman Catholic season of Lent, the 40-day period before Easter Sunday.

civil liberty—the right of people to do or say things that are not illegal without being stopped or interrupted by the government.

Communism—a political system in which all resources, industries, and property are considered to be held in common by all the people, with government as the central authority responsible for controlling all economic and social activity.

coup d'état—the violent overthrow of an existing government by a small group.

criollo—a resident of Spain's New World colonies who was born in North America to parents of Spanish ancestry. During the colonial period, criollos ranked above mestizos in the social order.

deforestation—the action or process of clearing forests.

economic system—the production, distribution, and consumption of goods and services within a country.

embargo—a government restriction or restraint on commerce, especially an order that prohibits trade with a particular nation.

foreign aid—financial assistance given by one country to another.

free trade—trade based on the unrestricted exchange of goods, with tariffs (taxes) only used to create revenue, not keep out foreign goods.

indigenous people—a name for native Amerindian tribes that lived in an area before Europeans came to settle there.

Latin America—a term for the areas of the American continents in which Spanish or Portuguese are the main languages. It includes nearly all of the Americas, except Canada, the United States, and a few small countries like Suriname and Guyana.

mestizo—a person of mixed Amerindian and European (typically Spanish) descent.

plaza—the central open square at the center of colonial-era cities in Latin America.

plebiscite—a vote by which the people of an entire country express their opinion on a particular government or national policy.

population density—a measurement of the number of people living in a specific area, such a square mile or square kilometer.

pre-Columbian—referring to a time before the 1490s, when Christopher Columbus landed in the Americas.

regime—a period of rule by a particular government, especially one that is considered to be oppressive.

Roman Catholicism—a Christian religion in which adherents obey the dictates of the Pope, whose headquarters is the Vatican in Rome. Roman Catholicism is the world's largest Christian denomination, with more than 1.2 billion members worldwide. Nearly 40 percent of Catholics live in Latin America.

service industry—any business, organization, or profession that does work for a customer, but is not involved in manufacturing.

Project and Report Ideas

Paraguayan Culture Box

Draw the flag of Paraguay on the lid of a shoebox. Paste pictures of Paraguay on the sides of the box. Find four to six items that reflect the culture of Paraguay and put them inside—these can include a CD of Paraguayan music, a book by a Paraguayan author, or craft items made by Paraguayan artisans. Write half a page explaining what each item is. Staple the pages together into a booklet with a cover and put it inside the box too.

Paraguayan Geography Map

Make a map of Paraguay. Draw in the Paraguay River, which divides the country into the Chaco and the Región Oriental. Put in the major cities. Color the forested areas green, the grassy plains red, and the dry areas yellow.

Paraguayan Animals and Ecology

Learn which animals live in the Chaco, which live in the forests of the Región Oriental, and which live in both. Get pictures of these animals and paste them into an album, organized by habitat.

Make *Ñandutí* with Paper

Find a picture of *ñandutí* lace. Trace or draw the pattern on a piece of paper. Then, using scissors, cut out around the lines you drew to make the paper look like lace.

How Big Is Itaipú?

The water reservoir at the Itaipú Dam is 106 miles (171 km) long and an average of 6 miles (9.7 km) wide. Get a map of your home area. With your hometown in the middle, draw a rectangle the size of the reservoir. What familiar landmarks would be underwater if the reservoir were really there?

Learn Guaraní and Spanish

Find out how to say "hello," "goodbye," "thank you," "please," "yes," and "no" in Spanish and in Guaraní. It shouldn't be hard to find Spanish translations, but Guaraní will be a challenge!

The U.S. and Paraguay in History

Look at the chronology of Paraguay's history. For each event listed, find out what major historical events were going on in the United States at the same time.

Asunción and American Cities

Make a list of all the U.S. cities that have a population similar to Asunción's, about 500,000 people. Find out which of those has an area similar in size to the Paraguayan capital.

Other Landlocked Countries

Paraguay has no access to the sea. Make a list of other countries in the world that are also landlocked. Write a report on the disadvantages they face.

1516	Alejo García becomes the first European to set foot in what is today Paraguay.
1537	Asunción is founded.
1609	Jesuits begin to establish Indian missions.
1617	Colonial government moved out of Asunción; city begins to decline.
1750	Treaty of Madrid, between Spain and Portugal, gives Brazil the Jesuit missions previously under Paraguayan protection.
1759	Portuguese king orders all Jesuits expelled from his empire.
1767	Spanish king orders all Jesuits expelled from his empire.
1767–1768	Joint Spanish-Portuguese military expeditions force Jesuit expulsion; some armed resistance by Jesuit-led Guaraní.
1811	Paraguay's Declaration of Independence is announced on May 15.
1813	Congress accepts national constitution written by José Gaspar Rodríguez de Francia.
1814–1840	Regime of José Gaspar Rodríguez de Francia.
1841–1862	Regime of Carlos Antonio López.
1864–1870	Paraguay is defeated in the War of the Triple Alliance, losing more than half its population and suffering six years of occupation by Argentina and Brazil after the fighting ends.
1932–1935	Paraguay fights and defeats Bolivia in the Chaco War.
1940–1949	Regime of General Higinio Morínigo.
1954	Alfredo Stroessner, an army general, takes power in a coup.
1984	Itaipú plant starts generating electricity.
1989	Stroessner is overthrown; General Andrés Rodríguez is elected president.
1992	A new democratic constitution is enacted.
1993	Juan Carlos Wasmosy becomes the first civilian elected president of

Paraguay under the new constitution.

1996 General Lino Oviedo launches an unsuccessful coup.

1998 After being elected president, Raúl Cubas tries to pardon Oviedo, provoking a constitutional crisis; Vice President Luis María Argaña, a critic of Cubas and Oviedo, is assassinated.

1999 Cubas resigns under threat of impeachment; Senate president Luis González Macchi succeeds him.

2001 Paraguayan and U.S. authorities crack down on alleged Muslim terrorist cells operating along tri-border region.

2002 González Macchi is formally charged with corruption; protests and a coup attempt are suppressed.

2003 Nicanor Duarte is elected president; González Macchi goes on trial for involvement in illegal bank transfers.

2004 Paraguay's soccer team wins an Olympic silver medal in Athens, Greece.

2006 Luis González Macchi is convicted of banking violations and sentenced to six years in jail.

2008 Fernando Lugo is elected president, ending over 60 years of Colorado Party rule.

2010 MERCOSUR member-states sign a free-trade agreement with Israel.

2012 In June, President Lugo is removed from office and his vice president, Federico Franco, is sworn in as president. Many countries condemn this action as a coup d'état, and MERCOSUR suspends Paraguay.

2013 Horacio Cartes is elected president.

2014 The Ache' people of Paraguay file a lawsuit claiming that the Stroessner government carried out a program of genocide against them.

Gilmette, John. *At the Tomb of the Inflatable Pig: Travels Through Paraguay.* New York: Vintage Books, 2005.

Hebblethwaite, Margaret. *Paraguay.* Chalfont St Peter, UK: Bradt Travel Guides, 2014.

Keen, Benjamin, and Keith Haynes. *A History of Latin America.* Boston: Wadsworth Cengage Learning, 2013.

Lambert, Peter, and Andrew Nickson, eds. *The Paraguay Reader.* Durham, N.C.: Duke University Press, 2013.

Williamson, Edwin. *The Penguin History of Latin America.* New York: Penguin Group, 2010.

Travel Information

http://gosouthamerica.about.com/od/paraguay/Paraguay.htm
http://travel.state.gov/travel/cis_pa_tw/cis/cis_997.html
http://www.interconnection.org/resources/paraguay.htm

History and Geography

http://www.paraguay.com
http://lcweb2.loc.gov/frd/cs/pytoc.html
http://www.state.gov/r/pa/ei/bgn/1841.htm

Economic and Political Information

https://www.cia.gov/library/publications/the-world-factbook/geos/pa.html
http://www.heritage.org/Index/country.cfm?id=Paraguay
www.oas.org/children/members/Paraguay.html

Caribbean/Latin American Action
1625 K Street NW, Suite 200
Washington, DC 20006
Phone: (202) 464-2031
Website: www.c-caa.org

Embassy of Paraguay
2400 Massachusetts Avenue N.W.
Washington, D.C. 20008
Phone: (202) 483-6960
Fax: (202) 234-4508
Website: www.mre.gov.py/embaparusa

U.S. Agency for International Development
Ronald Reagan Building
Washington, D.C. 20523-0001
Phone: (202) 712-0000
Website: www.usaid.gov
Email: pinquiries@usaid.gov

U.S. Department of Commerce
International Trade Administration
Office of Latin America and the Caribbean
1401 Constitution Ave., NW
Washington, D.C. 20230
Phone: (202) 482-2000
Fax: (202) 482-5168
Website: www.commerce.gov
Email: publicaffairs@doc.gov

Index

Contributors

Senior Consulting Editor **James D. Henderson** is professor of international studies at Coastal Carolina University. He is the author of *Conservative Thought in Twentieth Century Latin America: The Ideals of Laureano Gómez* (1988; Spanish edition *Las ideas de Laureano Gómez* published in 1985); *When Colombia Bled: A History of the Violence in Tolima* (1985; Spanish edition *Cuando Colombia se desangró, una historia de la Violencia en metrópoli y provincia*, 1984); and coauthor of *A Reference Guide to Latin American History* (2000) and *Ten Notable Women of Latin America* (1978).

Mr. Henderson earned a bachelor's degree in history from Centenary College of Louisiana, and a master's degree in history from the University of Arizona. He then spent three years in the Peace Corps, serving in Colombia, before earning his doctorate in Latin American history in 1972 at Texas Christian University.

Roger E. Hernández writes a syndicated column distributed to newspapers across the country by King Features, and is coauthor of *Cubans in America*, an illustrated history of the Cuban presence in the United States. He also teaches writing and journalism at the New Jersey Institute of Technology and Rutgers University.